Old Came Rectory

Dorset home of William Barnes

Thomas Hardy's mentor

Sedley Proctor

Old Came Rectory
First published in Great Britain by

Leopard Publishing Ventures Ltd
Hampshire SO212PR
www.thehalfdays.com
www.magickgate.com

A CIP catalogue record is available from the British Library.

ISBN: 978-0-9574550-6-1

Dedication

To the burrowers among the wild

Do not rage against the furious child

But with far flung feathery might

Bring forth old records into the light

Anon

Dedication

To the burrowers among the wild

Do not rage against the furious child

But with far flung feathery might

Bring forth old records into the light

Anon

Acknowledgements

In the research for this book I would like to thank Alan Chedzoy, author of *William Barnes, The People's Poet*, Brian Caddy and The William Barnes Society, Peter Monteith, archivist at King's College, Cambridge, Marion Tait and Mark North at the Dorset Museum, Joe Callahan of Chicago University, Jonathan Morrell, my writing and publishing partner, Tony Henderson, Phil Leach and Warren Davis whose enthusiasm and encouragement drove me on to unearth further curiosities surrounding the lovely old house in which they live.

Contents

Preface 3

The "Large Lofty Cottage" 5

William Barnes 8

Literary Visitors 16

A Hwomely Dwelling 26

The Rectory After Barnes 32

The Rectory Since the War 43

    Bibliography 47

Appendix 1...53

Appendix 2...57

    Photos and Drawings 59

Preface

To quote a slick purveyor of real estate there is "something quintessentially English," about rectories "which conjures up images of elegance, space and cucumber sandwiches on the lawn."[1]

The first time I visited Came Rectory it was winter and it was already getting dark outside. We were not served cucumber sandwiches on the lawn but rather a fruit cake in the living room.

"Have you read William Barnes?" inquired the American academic who was also visiting that day.

"No," I said, "I must confess all this is new to me. However, I have read some Thomas Hardy."

Living as I had abroad for a number of years, I saw all these things with a certain detachment and indeed amusement but also I think as someone who was happily in thrall to remembrance of things past.

---

[1] Quoted in Jennings, Anthony, *The Old Rectory*, Bloomsbury Publishing, 2009, P.9.

Later, I recall, I was given a tour of the house. Starting in what I was told had been the dining room in Barnes' day but was now the music room, everywhere I looked there were objects for the eye to feast on, particularly, as I noted in my diary:

> four little pictures on a brigand theme, some small romantic scenes of the Grand Tour, a drawing of Princess Charlotte, Queen to George IV; various prints from the Napoleonic era: Wellington surrounded by his troops, Napoleon on his way to St Helens... and in the dining room a portrait with a striking resemblance by my estimation to Wellington but I am assured is a French magistrate picked up in a Parisian flea market.

If I dwell on these details, there is a reason. It was as much the quintessentially English scene of tea in a rectory as all these pictures and *objets trouvés* that charmed and inspired me to begin my research into a house with such a rich architectural and literary heritage.

The "Large Lofty Cottage"[2]

Built to serve the benefices of Winterborne Came[3] and Whitcombe just outside Dorchester, Old Came Rectory was famously the home of Dorset dialect poet and philologist, the Reverend William Barnes (1801-86).

The present house, which replaced an earlier building near the parish church, was built for the Rev. Dr William England, who held the benefice between 1804 and 1836. In 1825, George Dawson Damer, heir to the Came Estate, married Mary "Minney" Seymour, the ward of Mrs. Fitzherbert (1757-1837), secret wife of the Prince Regent, later King George IV. Mrs. Fitzherbert allegedly settled a dowry of 20,000 on her ward and a further 20,000 was provided by the King. This considerable boost to the Estate coffers enabled the Dawson Damers to begin a lengthy programme of improvements which included the building of the new rectory. Although the architect has yet to be identified, it has been suggested that it is the work of, or, at the very least, copied from an architectural plan by a friend of the King, John Nash (1752-1835) who designed the first of many cottage orné.[4]

---

[2] Kilvert, Francis, *Kilvert's Diary*, ed. Plomer, William, Book Club Associates, London, 1986, P.255-60.

[3] The suffix Came relates to the manor being owned by the abbey of St. Stephen at Caen in Normandy from the time of William the Conqueror. Finchy, F.S., *The Dorset William Barnes*, The Dorset Bookshop, 1966, P.28.

[4] True English cottage orné style became popular after the Royal Lodge built by John Nash in Windsor Great Park, 1814. Billet, Michael, *Thatched Buildings of Dorset*, Hale Ltd, 1984, P.91-2.

The new rectory was built on the site of an earlier house known to be a withy man or basket maker's cottage.[5] The main façade facing west comprises three bays, and has a "hipped" valley thatched roof. In Barnes' words the "well-trimmed thatch" of the main house is complemented by three separate thatched verandas, supported by slender rustic poles made of yew.[67] The Rectory windows are a particularly striking feature of the design with their geometrical glazing bars, which follow a "Chinese" fretwork or tracery typical of the cottage orné made popular by Nash. If it was intended to appear as a Chinese chinois cottage orné, the Rectory was clearly conceived as a gentleman's residence with generously large corniced rooms. As a listed grade II building, the "shaggy-browed cottage" has been celebrated in both the pages of *Country Life* and academic review.[8][9][10]

Inside, the house has a relatively simple plan, with two reception rooms on the entrance façade and a stone-flagged hall leading, past a dining room and a drawing room, to a study for the Rector and the original kitchen, which is now the dining

---

[5] Evidence for this can be found in the three cellars situated along the northern axis of the rectory. Chedzoy, Alan, "Winterborne Came Rectory: the home of William Barnes", *Dorset Proceedings 123*, 2001.

[6] "Proud of his Home", quoted in Leader Scott (Lucy, Baxter), *The life of William Barnes, Poet and Philologist*, 1887, P.253-4.

[7] Billet, Michael, *Thatched Buildings of Dorset*, Hale Ltd, 1984, P.100-1.

[8] Listed 26/01/1956, English Heritage ID: 106005, www.britishlistedbuildings.co.uk.

[9] Motion, Andrew, *The William Barnes Society Newsletter*, No.42, May 2001, P.14.

[10] Brittain-Caitlin, Timothy, *Country Life*, 200, June 2006, P.114-6, ISSN00458856 and *The English Parsonage in the Early Nineteenth Century*, Shire Books, 2008, P.7.

room.[11][12] An elaborate balustrade ascends to a spacious landing serving five chambers. At the top of the Georgian well staircase is a long, narrow shelf where the Dorset poet, a keen collector of old paintings, was said to have cleaned his prints and pictures and where he was aided by the light from the landing, reflected in the lime washed walls of the coach house that stands to the east.[13][14] The original landing was extended when Barnes added a scullery to the kitchen downstairs with a corridor leading to a servant's bedroom above the scullery. The landing was also the place where Barnes' son, Miles, then rector of Monkton, arranged to play "several glees and madrigals" much to his bed-ridden father's delight:

 [He] clapped his hands, crying, "Bravi, bravi! – again, again!" His old favourite "By Celia's arbour", was one of those he would have repeated over and over again.[15]

---

[11] Bullen suggests the "symmetrical two-storied box" of Came Rectory is the model for Fitzpiers' house in *The Woodlanders*. Bullen, J. B., *Thomas Hardy, The World of His Novels*, Frances Lincoln Ltd, P116-7.

[12] The scullery, added early on by Barnes, is now a small kitchen.

[13] Leader Scott (Baxter, Lucy), *The life of William Barnes, Poet and Philologist*, 1887, P. 151-2.

[14] Barnes is thought to be the model for the rector in Hardy's poem, "The Collector Cleans his Picture."

[15] Leader Scott (Baxter, Lucy), *The life of William Barnes, Poet and Philologist*, 1887, P.320.

William Barnes

In 1862 the Rectory secured for itself a niche in British literary history as the home of the Rev. William Barnes, described by one of its visitors, the Rev. Francis Kilvert, as "the great idyllic poet of England."[16] Among Barnes' more enduring works, now best known in its musical setting by Vaughan Williams, is the poem, *My Orcha's in Linden Lea*. Barnes' "stray eclogues of rustic chat and challenge, between ploughmen, harvesters, (and) old 'commoners'" were to have a profound influence on the young Thomas Hardy.[17] Barnes' poems in both dialect and "Common English" are deceptively simple, often depending on a rhyming

---

[16] Kilvert, Francis, *Kilvert's Diary*, ed. Plomer, William, Book Club Associates, London, 1986, P.255-60.

[17] From "The Poet as Citizen" by Arthur Quiller-Couch quoted in Dugdale, Giles, *William Barnes of Dorset*, Cassell & Company, 1953, P.214-5.

couplet or an alternate rhyme scheme and a comic or pathetic turn of phrase:[18]

> Let other vo'k meäke money vaster
> In the aïr o' dark-room'd towns,
> I don't dread a peevish meäster;
> Though noo man do heed my frowns,
> I be free to goo abrode,
> Or teäke ageän my hwomeward road
> To where, vor me, the apple tree
> Do leän down low in Linden Lea.[19]

Barnes the Philologist

Barnes was not only a poet but also a noted philologist. If it sometimes feels like "entering a strange land, populated by clippings (consonants) and breathsounds (vowels)," an early admirer of Barnes' philological theories, the Jesuit poet, Gerald Manley Hopkins (1844-89) describes *An Outline of English Speech-Craft* (1878) as "the madness of an almost unknown man trying to do what the three estates of the realm could never accomplish."[20][21]

Barnes knew as many as seventy languages, among which "Hindustani, Persian, Arabic and other unwanted tongues."[22]

---

[18] Examples of both dialect and standard English poems are found in Leader Scott (Baxter, Lucy), *The life of William Barnes, Poet and Philologist*, 1887.

[19] Final stanza of "My Orcha'd in Linden Lea", Barnes, William, *Poems of Rural Life in the Dorset Dialect*, second edition, John Russell Smith, 1863.

[20] Leader Scott (Baxter, Lucy), *The life of William Barnes, Poet and Philologist*, 1887, P.137.

[21] Letter from Gerard Manley Hopkins to Robert Bridges, Nov 26 1882, quoted in Dugdale, Giles, *Life of William Barnes*, Cassell & Company, 1953, P.205.

[22] Treves, Sir Frederick, *Highways and Byways in Dorset*, Macmillan and Co, 1935, P. 16.

Testimony to his febrile polyglot imagination are the 150 psalms rendered from Hebrew in his own speech-craft and the score of poems translated from Farsi into standard English, preserved among his papers now in the Dorset museum:

> Here of wine, boy a measure, **bring** us out,
> Wine the purest that leaves the **wring**, give out;
>
> Wine that healeth the pain of love – a balm
> Fit for old, as for youth's gay **spring**, give out.
>
> Wine and glass, here to us, are sun and moon,
> So the sun for the moon's pale **ring**, give out.[23]

The Persian metre, illustrated here in Barnes' translation of Hafiz's Ode (1325/6-1389/90), known as the *ghazal*, a two-line verse with a rhyme at the end of each verse followed by an assonance, was also adopted by Barnes in his own poetry:

GREEN

> Our zummer way to church did wind about
> The cliff, where ivy on the **ledge** wer green.
>
> Our zummer way to town did skirt the wood,
> Where sheenèn leaves in tree an' **hedge** wer green.
>
> Our zummer way to milkèn in the mead
> Wer on by brook, where fluttrèn **zedge** wer green
>
> Our hwomeward ways did all run into one

---

[23] "A Persian Ode by Hafiz", first published, *The Dorset County Chronicle*, 1875, and later in *The Poems of William Barnes,* ed. Jones, Bernard, Centaur Classics, 1962.

Where moss upon the roofstwone's **edge** wer green.[24]

Barnes the Lecturer

Like many Victorians, Barnes was a meticulous recorder of his daily life, though, with a difference. He kept a journal in Italian in which he describes his everyday activities, often in his beloved garden, "zappando", or digging. One year (1855) he even switches to writing the journal in Spanish; another in Welsh, which his amused daughter claims to have been "rather untranslatable."[25]

While the keeping of a journal suggests a reflective man, Barnes also saw himself as a public writer. A regular contributor to the *Dorset County Chronicle*, he wrote for magazines such as *The Ladies Treasury* and *The Gentleman's Magazine* where, perhaps with a hint of self-mockery, he would sign himself: A Dilettante. Barnes' articles, however, were intended to instruct as well as to amuse. A tireless divulger and explicator, he would tour the working men's clubs both within and without the County, even if it was invariably his poetry recitals that drew the crowds:

> The hall was thronged almost to suffocation with rich and poor, and seldom has an audience been excited by various emotions… It seemed to one of the poet's children that the crowd of human beings was a magic harp on which he played, bringing forth at his will the emotions he chose.[26]

---

[24] "Woak Hill" and "Green" transcribed from Leader Scott (Baxter, Lucy*), The life of William Barnes, Poet and Philologist*, 1887, P.248.

[25] Leader Scott (Baxter, Lucy*), The life of William Barnes, Poet and Philologist*, 1887, P.160.

[26] Barnes' first recital for the Working Men's Institute in Dorchester Town Hall, 1860, Leader Scott (Baxter, Lucy), *The life of William Barnes, Poet and Philologist*, 1887, P. 167.

Described as "a keen thinker in social science and political economy,"[27] Barnes also wrote books on a range of academic subjects, including a history of Ancient Britain and an economic analysis of farm labour, as well as over nine hundred and fifty sermons, laid out in his insuperable scrapbooks, with capitals and dashes, like flashes of free verse:

> What is the Peace which Christ gives us – My peace I give unto you – It clears the Conscience – Hallows the Heart – Wins forgiveness of all sins.[28]

Barnes the School Master

If all this gives the impression that Barnes was something of a Renaissance man as well as a man of the cloth, he was also known to his contemporaries as an educationalist. For many years, aided by his wife, Julia Miles, Barnes ran a local school in Mere and later in Dorchester. As one of his biographers has pointed out, Barnes' teaching practices can be considered innovative and ahead of their time. Barnes placed great importance on the sciences, since these developed "reason and observation."[29]

A morning's study would begin with a short lecture, either as dictation or under the discipline of note taking. Experiments were conducted in physics and chemistry. Walks were made to encourage identification and classification in botany and geology:

> Sometimes the boys vied with each other who should find the greatest number of "Cruciferous" or "Composite flowers"; other days they went

---

[27] Preface, Leader Scott (Baxter, Lucy), *The life of William Barnes, Poet and Philologist*, 1887.

[28] Cited in Finchy, F.S., *The Dorset William Barnes*, The Dorset Bookshop, 1966, P.37-43.

[29] Leader Scott (Baxter, Lucy), *The life of William Barnes, Poet and Philologist*, 1887, P.48.

armed with hammers and bags for a geological expedition, finding specimens of terebratulae, echinus, or belemnite in the chalk cutting of the new railway.[30]

As with his children, Barnes rarely disciplined his pupils, but encouraged them to think through a course of action and then decide for themselves:

> The only visible register was an invention of the master's own, called the "topography". It consisted of a large flat box in which lay a board opposite each file of holes and painted in lines of colour – white, red, blue &c, and ending in black. The boy's names were placed at the top of the board opposite each file of holes, and according to his want of diligence the peg was moved down, only to be put up again on the completion of a voluntary task…To have one's peg in the "blues" caused the loss of a holiday; that a peg reached the "blacks" was a thing unheard of.[31]

If Barnes' method proved to be "more efficacious than canings and impositions," and the boys were kept at their best through a combination of conscience and peer pressure, Barnes' chief weapon was his ability to hold their interest. Describing a lecture on electricity one former pupil, J.B. Lock, who later became a lecturer in Mathematics and Physics at Cambridge, was moved to note "he gave us some sharp shocks with a frictional machine." Another, the parson naturalist and arachnologist of world renown, Octavius Pickard Cambridge (1828-1917) enthused about Barnes' "faculty of interesting his scholars, and not only causing them to understand but love what he taught."[32]

---

[30] Leader Scott (Baxter, Lucy), *The life of William Barnes, Poet and Philologist*, 1887, P.49.

[31]. Ibid., P.51-2.

[32] Quoted in Dugdale, Giles, *Life of William Barnes*, Cassell & Company, 1953, P.104.

Frederick Treves, the Victorian surgeon who once performed a life-saving operation on King Edward VII,[33] recalls, on the other hand, a gentle teacher, often wrapped in thought.

> I remember once, he wrote, that some forbidden fruit of which I was possessed rolled across the schoolroom floor, and that I crawled after it in the wake of the dreaming master. He turned suddenly in his walk and stumbled over me, to my intense alarm. When he had regained his balance he apologized very earnestly and resumed his walk unconscious that the object he had fallen over was a scholar. I have often wondered to which of his charming poems I owed my escape from punishment.[34]

After his wife's early death, the school in Dorchester went into decline. Help came, however, from an unexpected source. Invited by his former pupil, Seymour Dawson Damer to take up tenure at the Rectory, "the Dorset Burns" was also awarded a civil list pension of seventy pounds a year for his services to education.[35]

---

[33] After the then radical operation of draining the king's infected appendix, Treves was awarded a baronetcy and granted the use of the Thatched House Lodge in Richmond Park.

[34] Quoted in Mee, Arthur, *Dorset*, Hodder and Staughton, 1939, P.307.

[35] Under the application of the barrister, Frederick Cosens, Barnes' first pension did not arrive until the autumn of 1862. Hearl, T.W., *William Barnes, The Schoolmaster*, The Friary Press, Longmans, Dorchester, 1966, P.293-4.

Engraving of Woman Milking Cow by William Barnes, 1830s

Barnes the Engraver

Lastly and not least of his talents, the master and parson poet was also considered a "competent engraver" of country scenes on both wood and copper.[36]

**Research
William Barnes
Contact:**

The Curator
William Barnes Collection
Dorset County Museum
High West Street
Dorchester DTA1XA
secretary@dorsetcountymuseum.org

[36]Treves, Sir Frederick, *Highways and Byways in Dorset*, Macmillan and Co, 1935, P. 16.

Old Came Rectory with Laura Barnes in the foreground, 1880s

Literary Visitors

The growing literary fame of the "half hermit, half enchanter"[37] ensured a steady stream of visitors to Came Rectory during the years of Barnes' tenure (1862-86).

Two early visitors were the poets, Coventry Patmore (1823-96) and William Allingham (1824-89). Like Barnes, Coventry Patmore was recently widowed and had brought his eldest little daughter to visit the "haunts of the Blackmore Maidens" where:

> The primrose in the sheäde do blow,
> The cowslip in the zun,
> The thyme upon the down do grow,
> The clote (water-lily) where the streams do run[38]

---

[37] Kilvert, Francis, *Kilvert's Diary,* ed. Plomer, William, Book Club Associates, London, 1986, P.255-60.

[38] Leader Scott (Baxter, Lucy), *The life of William Barnes, Poet and Philologist,* 1887, P.218.

When Allingham came to stay in the spring of 1864, Barnes was cheerfully amused by the young poet, who spent much of his visit in "reckless correction of his proofs." Barnes himself made very few corrections "out of tender regard for his printers."[39]

Allingham also visited the Rectory with the Poet Laureate, Alfred, Lord Tennyson (1809-92). Late one night in 1867, on a walking tour, Tennyson and Allingham turned up at the Rectory where they were given supper and conversation before going on their way. Barnes insisted on leading his guest out into the early morning starlight and setting them on their road to Bridport and Lyme Regis.[40]

Kilvert's Visit

In April 1874, Barnes received a visit from the clergyman diarist, Francis Kilvert (1840-1879). Kilvert was met at Dorchester station by the vicar of Fordington, Henry Moule (1801-80),[41] who was also a formidable campaigner for improved sanitation.

The mid-Victorian years were beset by problems of overcrowding and disease. After the Great Stink of 1858, and following an outbreak of cholera in his own village, Moule would be inspired to invent the earth closet, which one can imagine, as in today's rural African communities,

---

[39] Leader Scott (Baxter, Lucy), *The life of William Barnes Poet and Philologist*, 1887, P.220.

[40] Dugdale, Giles, *William Barnes of Dorset*, Cassell & Company, 1953, P.184.

[41] The Moules are thought to be the models for the Clare family in *Tess of the D'Ubervilles*. Dugdale, Giles, *William Barnes of Dorset*, Cassell & Company, 1953, P.194-5.

occupying one of the outhouses at Came Rectory.

In his diary Kilvert records that he and Moule walked from Fordington to Came Rectory where Barnes received them as he was walking on the veranda in his study gown. Kilvert was much struck by Barnes' appearance, and particularly by the beauty and grandeur of his head:

> It was an apostolic head, bald and venerable, and the long, soft silvery hair flowed from his shoulders and a long white beard fell on his breast. His face was handsome and striking, keen yet benevolent, the finely pencilled eyebrows still dark and a beautiful, benevolent look lighted up his fine dark blue eyes when they rested on you.[42]

Inevitably the topic of conversation revolved around poetry. Kilvert records Barnes' explanation of how his poems came to him:

> He was born in Sturminster Newton, a son of a small farmer, and in his after life when he sat down to amuse himself by writing poetry, all the dear scenes and well-remembered events and beloved faces of his youth crowded upon his memory. "I saw them all distinctly before me," he said, "and all that I had to do was write them down. It was no trouble to me, the thoughts and words came of themselves."

After this, and much to Barnes' delight, Moule sang some verses in "a sweet, melodious voice" accompanying himself on the piano in the rectory drawing room. Kilvert records that Barnes then read some of his own poems:

> how worthy Bloom the Miller went to London to see the great "glassen house" and how he could not get into the omnibus by reason of his bulk… We were all three in roars of laughter. Then to please me he read his beautiful poem "Happiness". He read in a low voice, rather indistinct

---

[42] Kilvert, Francis, *Kilvert's Diary*, ed. Plomer, William, Book Club Associates, London, 1986, P.255-60.

and with much feeling. "I like your pathetic pieces best," said the vicar. "So do I," said the poet.[43]

Hardy at Max Gate

In 1883, Hardy built his own house, Max Gate, a short distance from Came Rectory, chosen with Barnes' help for its archaeological interest.[44] Thereafter, Hardy was a frequent visitor at the Rectory. With him, on July 23 1883, came Edmund Gosse (1849-1928) who, like Kilvert before him, noted Barnes' "long silky white hair flowing down and mingling with a full beard and moustache also as white as milk a grand dome of a forehead over a long thin pendulous nose."

> His dress is interesting, black knee breeches and silk stockings, without gaiters, and buckled shoes.[45]

Barnes, it must be pointed out, had his own unique sense of fashion, or what he called "prinking", based on utility and comfort. Another favoured outdoor garment was the "poncho" made of Scotch plaid, or the Basque cap brought by his friend Mr. Colfox from the Pyrenees.[46]

Barnes had many literary friendships during his long life, notably with Caroline Norton (1808-77), poetess and granddaughter of the playwright, Richard Brinsley Sheridan, and the nephew of the emperor, Prince Lucien Bonaparte

---

[43] Kilvert, Francis, *Kilvert's Diary,* ed. Plomer, William, Book Club Associates, London, 1986, P.255-60.

[44] For a discussion of the building of Max Gate, see Millgate, Michael, *Thomas Hardy, A biography*, 1982, P.249, P.257.

[45] Quoted in Chedzoy, Alan, *William Barnes, Life of Dorset Poet*, Dovecote Press Ltd, 1985, P.173.

[46] Leader Scott (Baxter, Lucy), *The life of William Barnes Poet and Philologist*, 1887, P.209.

(1813-1891) with whom he conducted a correspondence regarding matters philological.[47] In his later years, however, champions and admirers of his work such as the young Oxfordian Arthur Quiller Couch (1863-1944) came from far and wide. Among the last of his literary contemporaries to visit Barnes was the author of *The Golden Treasury*, Francis Turner Palgrave (1824-97) who still found him "bright in mind and eye – as he must have been his youth, but full of the ripe experience of a long life."[48]

Although not documented, it is thought that the Scottish writer Robert Louis Stevenson (1850-94), who visited Max Gate in August 1885, may also have visited Came Rectory since it was Hardy's custom, as it had been with Gosse, to bring his guests over to meet Barnes.

---

[47] Barnes had translated the Song of Solomon into Dorset dialect for Bonaparte's book celebrating local dialects. Leader Scott (Baxter, Lucy), *The life of William Barnes, Poet and Philologist*, 1887, P.183.

[48] Dugdale, Giles, *William Barnes of Dorset*, Cassell & Company, 1953, P.232.

Thomas Hardy in middle age; William Barnes in his Basque cap, 1870s

Barnes and Hardy

In spite of the forty-year difference in age between Barnes and Hardy, there was great affection and durability in the friendship that was forged between the two.

As a young man, Thomas Hardy (1840-1928) had worked as an apprentice architect in South Street, Dorchester, next door to Barnes' school. Florence Emily Hardy's memoirs describe how the young Hardy would run over to the school room to consult Barnes on some "knotty" point of grammar.[49] If, however, he was the pupil to Barnes' master, Hardy recalls with relish "the droll delivery of such pieces as "The Shy Man", "A bit o' sly Courten" and "Dick and I" that infuses Barnes' readings around the town-halls of the Shire."[50]

---

[49] Chedzoy, Alan, *William Barnes, A Life of the Dorset Poet*, Dovecote Press Ltd, 1985, P.139.

[50] Quoted in Dugdale, Giles, *William Barnes of Dorset*, Cassell & Company, 1953, P.160.

At this time, one might define their relationship as that of a younger man seeking the advice and approval of an older man whose poetry he greatly admired.[51] It was not only, however, the poet Hardy admired, but also the man. Writing in *The Athenaeum* after Barnes's death, Hardy states "a more notable example of self-help has seldom been recorded."[52] From yeoman's son to schoolmaster and then rector, it could be argued that Barnes climbed as high as a man of his birth could be expected in Victorian society.

If the idea of a life as a parson poet had not been unattractive to Hardy, returning later from London to settle, he would not forget the charismatic poet of his roots. Indeed, Hardy was a regular visitor at Came Rectory during the eighteen sixties and seventies, and more intensely, after the building of Max Gate, in the last few years of Barnes' life.[53]

At this time of life Barnes walked everywhere between his church at Winterborne Came and Whitcombe, often twice a day, and in all weathers. Hardy describes how, on his regular walk into Dorchester, invariably on Wednesday or Saturday market days, accompanied by his little, grey dog, Barnes would keep to the middle of the street, meditating as he walked.[54] His first

---

[51] For the influence on Hardy of Barnes' metrical experiments and Wessex world view, see Dugdale, Giles, *William Barnes of Dorset*, Cassell & Company, 1953, P. 191 -7.

[52] Ibid., P.3.

[53] Chedzoy, Alan, *The People's Poet, William Barnes of Dorset*, the History Press, 2010, P.174.

[54] Hardy, Thomas, "The Reverend William Barnes B.D.," *The Athenaeum*, October 16, 1886.

action on reaching the centre was to set his watch by the clock that gave reliable Greenwich meantime.[55]

Drawn together by mutual interests in literature, local archaeology, folklore and rural customs, the younger and older man might easily have clashed over beliefs. Like many of his contemporaries, Hardy's religious beliefs had been knocked by the evolutionary theories of Darwin. For Barnes, however, religion was a matter of faith and not intellect; indeed, Barnes would rarely involve himself in the doctrinal debates that gnawed at the heart of the Victorian Church. As one of Barnes' biographers has suggested, there was a tacit agreement not to bring up contentious subjects. On Barnes' part there is no record of criticism of Hardy's "agnosticism" or "pessimism", or as Hardy himself preferred it, his "evolutionary meliorism."[56]

Writing of Hardy's visits to Came Rectory in Barnes' old age, Barnes' daughter notes:

> Many a talk and laugh did the Dorset poet and the novelist have over old Dorset characters and bygone phrases of country life. Among these William Barnes might recall the honest old Vale farmer, who, seeing his neighbour's daughters going to her music lessons, said to him: "Goin' to spank the pianner at milking time! And it did indeed come to something, for they became bankrupt.[57]

Their friendship, if not based on shared views, was one of shared heritage and temperament. As children both men had been physically frail; in the wake of suffering, after the loss of loved ones, both men grew excessively fond of animals.

---

[55] Cited in Dugdale, Giles, *William Barnes of Dorset*, Cassell & Company, 1953, P.220.

[56] Ibid., P. 196.

[57] Leader Scott (Baxter, Lucy), *The life of William Barnes, Poet and Philologist*, 1887, P.278.

Pets were welcome members of the Barnes and Hardy households. Hardy's love of cats and dogs is well-documented both in poetry and prose and borne out by the presence of the cemetery dedicated to his pets at Max Gate. In his later years, Barnes' dog, Cara accompanied him on his country walks, or lay curled up at his feet "when he sat dreaming under the shadows in his corner by the hop vine."

"THE DOG WI' ME.

Aye then as I did straggle out
To your house, oh! How glad the dog
Wi' lowset nose did nimbly jog
Along my path, an' hunt about,
An' his main pleasure wer' to run
Along by boughs, or timber'd brows;
An' ended where my own begun
At your wold door and stwonèn floor.

An' there, wi' time a-glidèn by,
Wi' me so quick, wi' him so slow,
How he did look at me, an' blow;
Vrom time to time a whinèn sigh;
A-meanèn – "Come now let us goo
Along the Knolls wi' rabbit holes;
I can't think what you have to do
Wi' theäse young feäce, in theäse wold pleäce."[58]

---

[58] Like Hardy with his dog Wessex, Barnes dedicates the poem "The Dog Wi' Me" to his dog, Cara. Leader Scott (Baxter, Lucy), *The life of William Barnes Poet and Philologist*, 1887, P.283-4.

Domestic Staff at Came Rectory, Mrs. Charles, the cook, centre, ca 1880; Laura Barnes; William Barnes' grandchildren, Ethel and Arthur

A Hwomely Dwelling

Writing under the *nom de plume*, Leader Scott, Barnes' daughter, Lucy Baxter compares Old Came Rectory to "a cosy little nest" where on the wide eaves and the rustic pillars of the wider veranda "roses, clematis, and honeysuckle entwine". Photographs from the poet's era show "the flowery lawn in front", decorated with small conifers and pampas grass, with "a sheltering veil of trees at the side."[59]

Lucy describes the view from the poet's study on the upper floor, which overlooks "the sunny fruit garden" (the walled garden) where Barnes could "watch the blossoms expanding

---

[59] Leader Scott (Baxter, Lucy), *The life of William Barnes, Poet and Philologist*, 1887, P.199.

and falling from his apple and apricot trees" and see "the breezes waving his feathery-headed asparagus."[60]

Barnes himself describes the view beyond the garden from his study window where, "on a ridge of ground", he can see "a very fine old British Barrow burial tumulus with a clump of trees growing on it."[61]

The reference is to Conquer Barrow, just east of Hardy's home, Max Gate, which is today obscured by trees.[62] Barnes' passion for archaeology is reflected in the presence, in the orchard, of Sarsen stones unearthed during the repair of the walled garden in the 1990s.

The Walled Garden

When work began on the restoration of the walled garden, the present owners looked to respect the ordinance map of the 1880s which showed the area within the walls divided into four quarters by walks. The foundations of an old summerhouse were found to be aligned on the sitting room window. On the advice of the late Rosemary Verey (1918-2001), garden designer and historian, a circular pool was essential at the intersection of the four paths; such a pool, confirmed by the ordinance survey, was a common feature of Victorian walled gardens. A dowser was also employed to unearth the roots of the old trees in the orchard.

---

[60] Leader Scott (Baxter, Lucy), *The life of William Barnes, Poet and Philologist*, 1887, P.199.

[61] Letter to Daniel Ricketson of New Bedford, Massachusetts, Hinchy, F.S., *The Dorset William Barnes*, Dorset Bookshop, 1966, P.27.

[62] Barnes was one of the "foster fathers" of the Dorset County Museum. Leader Scott (Baxter, Lucy), *The life of William Barnes, Poet and Philologist*, 1887, P.89-93.

In a letter to one of his American correspondents, Barnes writes of his pleasure in the coming of spring and summer:

> May is a charming month, in which our dry downs are covered with sheets, as it were of silver and gold, in daisies and buttercups. June is our hay month. We are rich in wild flowers: the snowdrop comes in January; daffodils are now going off, and primroses are now coming into full bloom, and will soon be followed by cowslips and anemones or windflowers. On the Frome in May will bloom in snow-white patches the water crowfoot, or water ranunculus, a charming sight, with the water tinted blue from the sky, as it is given in my little poem, "White and Blue". The river Stour bears the yellow water-lily, Nurphur Lutea, which we call the clote. Our hedges, as the summer goes on, are tinted with the blossom of the blackthorn, whitethorn, honeysuckle, wild rose, and briony, goosegrass, and other plants.[63]

The new garden contains many of Barnes' favourite plants such as the fruit trees and "feathery" asparagus and, most importantly, white roses. Barnes' wife, Julia Miles died before he moved to Came Rectory.[64] Yet, just as he did in verse, Barnes sought to preserve Julia's memory in the white scented rose brought from their home in Dorchester:

> An' wi' a rosebud's mossy ball,
>
> I decked your bosom vrom the wall[65]

To the end of his life Barnes took a deep and abiding pleasure in his garden:

> His favourite dreaming place was a certain corner of the lawn at Came, where in May a red hawthorn tree and flowering laburnum mingled their

---

[63] Leader Scott (Baxter, Lucy), *The life of William Barnes, Poet and Philologist, 1887*, P.345.

[64] In the living room at Came Rectory hangs an oil portrait said to be the wife of William Barnes; described by Duke's Auctioneers as English School ca 1830 and, according to the label on the reverse, once the property of the poet's grandson, Colonel Lawrence Barnes.

[65] "The Wold Wall", quoted in Leader Scott (Baxter, Lucy), *The life of William Barnes, Poet and Philologist*, 1887, P.122.

shades on the grass, and feathery tamarisks, syringe and lilac blossomed in the sheltering shrub behind.[66]

On the outside of the walled garden, facing south-west, is a traditional Purbeck stone bench. As the warmest corner of the garden, it seems the most likely spot for Barnes' "dreaming place." From here Barnes could also keep an eye open for guests that might appear at the gate.

After wedding of Isabel Shaw (nee Barnes) to Thomas Gardener, 17 October, 1882: Constance, Reverend William Barnes, Arthur on donkey (Tom?), Harry Gardner, Ethel, Aunt Laura, Annette Gardner and (?)

---

[66] Leader Scott (Baxter, Lucy), *The life of William Barnes, Poet and Philologist*, 1887, P.247.

The Geate a-vallen to

Something of this rural idyll is encapsulated by a photograph of the clergyman "surrounded by his women folk and by his son – William Miles Barnes, also a clergyman in a shovel hat with a long beard, echoed in the elegiac note of the old man's final verses "a regret for a way of life which will never come again":

> An' oft do come a saddened hour
> When there must goo away
> One well-beloved to our heart's core,
> Vor long, perhaps vor aye:
> An' oh! It is a touchen thing
> The loven heart must rue,
> To hear behind his last farewell
> The geate a-vallen to[67]

During his final illness, confined "in cardinal scarlet in his white bed," Barnes was most concerned that the gate should not be closed.[68] Indeed, the gate should remain open to all.[69] It was finally closed after the cortege left for his funeral witnessed by Hardy and other eminent literary mourners:

> The clang of the gate behind the simple procession when the poet passed out of his home for the last time fell with a deep meaning on some of the mourners' hearts.[70]

---

[67] Wilson A. N., *The Victorians*, Hutchinson, 2002, P.430.

[68] Edmund Gosse's letter to Coventry Patmore describing Hardy's and his visit to the dying Barnes is quoted in full in Dugdale, Giles, *William Barnes of Dorset*, Cassell & Company, 1953, P.229.

[69] Dictated to Laura Barnes after Francis Turner Palgrave's visit in October, 1886, Dugdale, Giles, *William Barnes of Dorset*, Cassell & Company, 1953, P.221-4.

[70] Leader Scott (Baxter, Lucy), *The life of William Barnes, Poet and Philologist*, 1887, P 326.

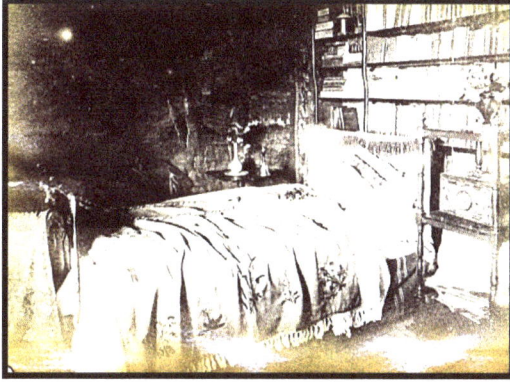

William Barnes' bed, shortly after his death

After he attended Barnes' funeral in October 1886, Hardy was moved to write "The Last Signal" as a tribute to his friend. In the second stanza the gate assumes a symbolic significance:

> Then amid the shadow of that livid east,
> Where the light was least, and a gate stood wide,
> Something flashes the fire of the sun that was facing it,
> Like a brief blaze on that side.[71]

In the final fourth stanza Hardy again draws the parallel between the physical gate through which Barnes passed during his busy parochial life and his entry into eternity:

> To take his last journey forth – he who in his prime
> Trudge so many a time from that gate athwart the land!
> Thus a farewell to me he signalled on his grave-way;
> As with a wave of his hand[72]

---

[71] Dugdale suggests the hidden rhymes in "The Last Signal" are a tribute to Barnes' metrical experiments. Dugdale, Giles, *William Barnes of Dorset*, Cassell & Company, 1953, P.231.

[72] "The Last Signal", *Collected Poems of Thomas Hardy*, Wordsworth Poetry Library, 1994.

The Rectory After Barnes

Shortly after his death, Barnes' property was put up for auction. Intriguingly, the record of the auction shows that Hardy bought two paintings from Barnes' collection.[73]

While today the whereabouts of these two paintings is unknown, one has cause to wonder: might they not have been two of the "worthy" canvases celebrated in Hardy's poem of the rural parson who is imagined delving in the back-rooms of Dorchester to uncloak some neglected masterpiece, "blacked blind by uncouth adventure."[74]

After the auction, Barnes' unmarried daughter, Laura, who had been his housekeeper and nursemaid at the end, was obliged to move out of the Rectory.[75] In the years following Barnes' death, however, Came Rectory remained the home of the Rector of Winterborne Came. His immediate successor was the unfortunately named Rev. William Ernest Evill, who was in turn succeeded by the Rev. Herbert John Underhill Charlton and the Rev. S. Homan.

In 1999 a commentary on the latter two gentlemen was found by the present owners on an unexpected source. On the

---

[73] Small landscape with trees and one other landscape with figures, Lot 295, "*Came Rectory*, Sale of Household Furniture, the property of the late Rev. Barnes," Nov 26, 1886.

[74] "The Collector Cleans His Pictures," *The Collected Poems of Thomas Hardy*, Wordsworth Poetry Library, 1994.

[75] Laura Barnes was granted the continuance of Barnes' Civil List Pension on the petition of the poets Robert Browning, Matthew Arnold, Francis Palgrave and other admirers of her father's work. Dugdale, Giles, *William Barnes of Dorset*, Cassell & Company, 1953, P. 228.

under-side of rear landing floorboards an inscription was written in pencil by workmen repairing the floors:

> Mr Walter Geoffrey
> JG Palmer
> R House
> J H Geoffrey
> Laid this floor May 8th 1896
> (?) Charlton resigned this living after getting drunk (bad wine?) and worse come that was the Rev. Claud Homan he don't get drunk but he is interfearing with every bodys livings.
> So much for parsons like these all of them ought to get 6 months in a shit house head downwards.
> So help my (?)[76]

Edmund Blunden, ca 1914; Siegfried Sassoon, 1915

The War Poets Come to Came

History does not record if there were notable guests at Came Rectory during the intervening years.

---

[76] For the transcript of the evidence from the floorboards and related information the present owners are grateful to Mr. Jonathan Lovie of the Garden History Society.

The tradition of literary visitors begun, however, in Barnes' time lived on when the war poet, Siegfried Sassoon (1886-1967) and his good friend, Edmund Blunden (1896-1974) came to stay at the Rectory as paying guests in the summer of 1923.[77] Sassoon, who kept a diary of the visit, records that he actually stayed in the room where Barnes had passed away, noting that it was a month before he was born.[78]

In his diary Sassoon is somewhat dismissive of the then occupant of Came Rectory. His host was the Reverend W. Godber, who was a padre in the Great War. Sassoon writes with evident distaste for the Rector's conversation with his stereotypical references to the "lads in France", "spirit of 1914", and the "decline of the old-fashioned (hat-touching?) agricultural labourer."

Sassoon's attitude to the war padre's jingoism is perhaps understandable. Although decorated for bravery, Sassoon had objected to the war and the senseless slaughter, castigating the politicians who had prolonged the conflict for their own duplicitous ends.

> "On behalf of those who are suffering now," he wrote in his famous *Soldier's Declaration*, "I make this protest about the deception that is being practised upon them; also I believe that I may help to destroy the callous complacence with which the majority of those at home regard the continuance of agonies which they do not share, and which they do not have the imagination to realise."[79]

---

[77] From a letter dated 5 April 1959, among Bernard Jones' papers, held in the archives of the Dorset Museum.

[78] *Siegfried Sassoon's Diaries*, 1923-5, ed. Hart Davies, Rupert, P. 51-3.

[79] Read before the House of Commons, July 30 1917, printed in *The London Times*, July 31, 1917, ironically on the first day of the Third Battle of Ypres, Passchendaele. Quoted in Graves, Robert, *Goodbye to All That*, Penguin Classics, P.213-4.

Blunden's attitude to the war, which he would evoke so memorably in his autobiographical account, *The Undertones of War*, was not dissimilar but perhaps more nuanced. Blunden who, like Sassoon, had been decorated and received the Military Cross describes the Passchendaele drive of 1917 as "murder not only to the troops but their singing faiths and hopes."[80]

Nevertheless, if there were objections to the war padre, Blunden and Sassoon's stay appears to have been comfortable and perhaps even imbued with a certain nostalgia for that "country rectory quietude" Blunden had stumbled upon, freakishly, in a break from battle.[81]

> Summer had even greater liberty than usual to multiply his convolvulus, his linnets and butterflies… {and} an unexampled simplicity of desire awoke in the imagination and rejoiced like Ariel in a cow-slip bell.[82]

Some twenty years later, Blunden would dedicate his book on Hardy to Sassoon, "remembering other days in the homes of William Barnes and Thomas Hardy."[83] The main purpose of Sassoon and Blunden's stay was, of course, to visit Barnes' old friend, Hardy, who was revered by the young poets.

Sassoon records that they visited the Hardys at Max Gate for tea on the 28th July. Hardy is "charming and alert"; his friend EB (Blunden) is "intent, respectful and bird-like," while Hardy tells them about the one act play he is writing for the Dorchester

---

[80] From Edmund Blunden's foreword to *Up the Line to Death*, The War Poets, 1914-1918, ed. Gardner, Brian, Metheun, 1964.

[81] Sassoon describes watching the rain over William Barnes "old thatched cottage", while they read leisurely in the mornings. *Siegfried Sassoon's Diaries*, 1923-5, ed. Hart Davies, Rupert, P 51-3.

[82] Blunden, Edmund, *The Undertones of War*, 1928, Penguin Classics, P.24.

[83] Cited in Ronald D., *TE Lawrence and his Circle*, Knight, Bat and Ball Press, 1988, P.53.

Players. This turns to be "The Famous Tragedy of the Queen of Cornwall", which would be performed in Dorchester later that year. Hardy offers to read from it; Sassoon is amused; Florence Hardy suggests in an aside that "reading is not one of {her husband's} strong points."

Sassoon is again amused when another tea guest described as a fashionable beauty gushes about Hardy's novels:

> Hardy shuts her up by saying "I'm not interested in my novels. I wrote them over 30 years ago."[84]

While Sassoon writes as if permanently amused, the impression he himself gives to other members of the party at Max Gate is of one "not ill-mannered but rather unmannered, lolling on the couch reading and ostentatiously ignoring us, non-existent for spells, except for a slight and refined snort."[85]

T.E Lawrence on his Brough Superior, 1920s

---

[84] Lady Stacie, a descendant, Sassoon notes, of the playwright Richard Brinsley Sheridan whose granddaughter, Caroline Norton, Barnes had known some fifty years before. *Siegfried Sassoon's Diaries*, 1923-5, ed. Hart Davies, Rupert, P 51-3.

[85] Secretary, May O'Rourke quoted in Ronald D., *TE Lawrence and his Circle*, Knight, Bat and Ball Press, 1988, P.53.

The Third Guest

In a letter to the Barnes scholar, Bernard Jones, in the late 1950s Sassoon alludes to a third guest staying at Came Rectory in the summer of 1923. Though not mentioned by name in the letter, it is clear from Sassoon's diaries that it was T.E. Lawrence (1888-1935).

After the First World War Lawrence had returned to Britain a hero. The Lawrence of Arabia who had acted as advisor to the Emir Faisal during the Paris Peace Talks (1919) and was famously painted by Augustus John in his Arab robes and headgear was, however, disgusted with his fame, and perhaps disgusted with himself. Afflicted by "mind-suicide" and "self-degradation," Lawrence signed up to the tank regiment at Bovington Camp, living under a pseudonym, first as R.H. Ross and then as T.E. Shaw.[86] During his time off from the camp it was Lawrence's custom to visit the Hardys, with whom he had become good friends.

In his diary Sassoon relates a comic episode involving Lawrence. Expected at tea; Lawrence is late when he turns up in his side-car, leaves a message with one of the servants and shoots off again. Sassoon catches up with him at the gate. "He looked well," records Sassoon, "a queer little figure in dark motor overalls, his brown and grimy face framed in a fur-line cap."[87]

On the twenty-ninth, the following day, Lawrence returns for lunch with Sassoon and Blunden at Came Rectory. Sassoon

---

[86] In a letter to Lionel Curtis, 1923, cited in Orlans, Harold, *T.E. Lawrence: Biography of a Broken Hero*, McFarland, 2002, P.62.

[87] *Siegfried Sassoon's Diaries*, 1923-5, ed. Hart Davies, Rupert, P 51-3.

records that Lawrence stayed with them from one o'clock to six thirty. In that time, they again visit the Hardys for tea. Sassoon writes that Blunden made notes of their conversations, but, disappointingly, he does not trouble to record them in his diary. Yet, from his letter to Jones, we know that one of the likely topics of conversation was William Barnes. Sassoon implies that E.B. (Blunden) was the one who really knew Barnes' poetry, though tellingly Sassoon must have been impressed by what he learnt during the week they spent at the Rectory. In a final note to Jones, Sassoon writes that his own copy of Barnes' poems had belonged to Edward Fitzgerald, the Victorian poet who had translated *The Rubáiyát of Omar Khayyám* (1859):

The Moving Finger writes: and, having writ,
Moves on[88]

The Rylands at Came

Like Lawrence, Sassoon was to become one of the Hardy watchers who would call upon the venerated poet during the final years of his life. Hardy died in 1928. Florence Hardy continued to live at Max Gate until her own death in 1937.

Among the many visitors to Max Gate in the mid to late twenties was a young man fresh from Cambridge, George "Dadie" Rylands (1902-99).

From the 1930s to the early 1950s Came Rectory was home to Dadie's mother, Betha Rylands.[89] Betha Rylands was a

---

[88] From Quatrain 51, *The Rubáiyát of Omar Khayyam*, Fitzgerald, Edward, 1859.

[89] Betha Rylands is listed as a private resident of Came Rectory in *Kelly's Directory of Dorsetshire*, 1935, Kelly's Directories Ltd, High Holborn.

clergyman's widow. On her mother's side, she was related to a well-known West Stafford family. Betha's great aunt was Evangeline E. Smith, daughter of Reginald Southwell Smith, who had been rector at West Stafford. Friend to the Barnes children, Evangeline was an aspiring novelist who had sought advice from Hardy on the art of short story writing and would publish several novels in her lifetime, notably, and perhaps in homage to the master, *A Cruel Necessity* (1886).[90]

"Dadie" Rylands

Betha's son, "Dadie" is an interesting figure in his own right who, on the evidence of his personal archive bequeathed to King's College, Cambridge, spent a lifetime cultivating friends and influence. A leading Shakespeare scholar and fellow of King's College Cambridge, Dadie counted as friends the doyens of the Bloomsbury set, the historian Lytton Strachey (1880-1932) and the writer Virginia Woolf (1882-1941).

Dadie lived in the same set of rooms at Kings from 1927, when he was a junior fellow until the time of his death. These rooms were the scene of a lunch party described in Woolf's *A Room of One's Own*. The luncheon "began with soles, sunk in a deep dish, over which the college cook had spread a counterpane of whitest cream, save that it was branded here and there with brown spots like the spots on the flanks of a doe."[91]

---

[90] From an explanatory note appended by Rylands to an article "Thomas Hardy and Evangeline F Smith" by Bath M.E. in *The Hardy Yearbook*, 1974, P.36-47. The Rylands Archive, King's College, Cambridge GWR/MISC.

[91] Woolf, Virginia, *A Room of One's Own*, Oxford World Classics, New Edition, 2015, P. 8.

Together with Maynard Keynes (1883-1946), Dadie would found the Cambridge Arts Theatre of which he was to be chairman between 1946 and 1982. The Arts Theatre was home to the Cambridge University Marlowe Society where Dadie directed many well-received productions of Shakespeare's works. Through the society and his role as chairman of the Arts Theatre he would help nurture the careers of post-war actors such as Ian MacKellen and Derek Jacobi, and the theatre directors, Peter Hall and Trevor Nunn.[92]

If these are the bare facts of Dadie's biography, from the Rylands archive kept at King's College, Cambridge, an impression emerges of Dadie's intense academic life during the thirties and forties. Yet, while deeply involved in his teaching and undergraduate theatrical productions, often, in the holidays, he would retreat to his mother's home at Came Rectory where life seemed to go on much as it had done before, in Barnes like contemplation, country walks and picnics.[93]

Betha, like Barnes before her, appears to be a keen gardener. She cultivates her own kitchen garden and enjoys making her own jams and cheeses.[94] The tone of her correspondence with Dadie is affectionate and appreciative of her busy son. If, around this time, she begins to feel her age, and her fading sight, and will refer to herself as the invalid, it is not as an invalid she

---

[92] Cribb T.J., "Obituary: George Rylands." *The Independent*, 20 January, 1999.

[93] In a letter to Lady Ann Barnes (no relation of William Barnes' family), August 1940, Dadie describes just such a picnic on Egdon Heath above Hardy's cottage at Higher Bockhampton. The Rylands Archive, King's College, GHWR/MISC/83,1933-82.

[94] A guest writes to pass on his thanks for a much appreciated Christmas present of honey and damson cheese, "a better conserve he had not tasted." The Rylands Archive, King's College, Cambridge, GHWR/3/24.

writes. Instead, she fills her letters with news of Dorset, of an aunt living in Portland, of local Dorset friends and acquaintances. The effect is rather charming. Certainly Dadie appears attentive. He writes often and at length to involve his mother in his academic and literary pursuits. Meanwhile, she looks forward to his visits, as do the staff at Came Rectory.

Came During the War

This feeling intensifies in the letters written after 1939. The heavenly days of summer experienced by one guest at Came in the thirties would appear to recede in the fog and uncertainty of the times. [95] While Dadie's war effort is conducted on the home front from Kings, Betha's other son, James is at sea. The convoys under attack from U-boats in the Atlantic are often in her thoughts, as are the reports from the Admiralty. Out in the Channel she hears guns at intervals, some exchange, she supposes, between the Navy and a German ship that has strayed too close to the coastal defences, not unlike, one imagines, the guns that troubled Hardy in his First World War poem, "Channel Firing":

> Again the guns disturbed the hour,
> Roaring their readiness to avenge,
> So far inland as Stourton Tower,
> And Camelot, and starlit Stonehenge.[96]

---

[95] In a letter to Dadie Rylands from Lady Ann Barnes, summer of 1935. The Rylands Archive, King's College, Cambridge, GHWR/3/23/1.

[96] Quoted in *Up the Line to Death*, The War Poets 1914-1918, anthology by Gardener B., foreword by Blunden, Edmund, Metheun, 1964.

If, however, the war appears to be coming to Camelot and indeed Came, there remain for Betha the comforts of her home and more particularly, as for the grieving Barnes before her, of her garden.

Writing in the summer months of 1942, Betha appears to make light of her preoccupations.

May 12: she is expecting guests. "I have no meat" she laments, "but I shall feed them on curried eggs and a delicious pudding of sorts called New Year's Pudding but set not your heart on it our last raisins are going into it." She delights in the Clematis Montana, "you can't put a pin between the flowers," and tells Dadie she has set aside the lilies of the valley to be put in the post.

May 22: Betha is sorry to see the end of the pheasant eye narcissus and tulips. Enthusing, however, about the strawberries and cherries, "the sweet ones by the paddock,", she is also expecting honey, in contrast to the previous year when they got none, and describes with delight the swarming of the bees. How she hopes the queen bees will sort it out once they get back to their hive!

June 20: Promising to do all little Dutch hoeing before he comes down, Betha beseeches Dadie to tell Maynard (Keynes) "that you have an invalid mother who is counting the days till you return."

July 29: full of local and family news, Betha invokes the censor of Eileen (the Housekeeper), fresh from planting 400 leeks to "tell Mr George to come home soon or he will not taste peas."

September 18: Dadie has been and gone, and presumably eaten the peas. Amid the news from the Admiralty and the convoys in the Atlantic, Betha is happy to note the marigolds and monkshood are out on the borders.[97]

The Rectory Since the War

Betha Rylands, who "delighted and startled us for the cracks we thought safely out of her range," died in 1953.[98]

For a while Came Rectory was rented by H.O.B. Duke of the company of Hy Duke auctioneers from his uncle, Rev. W. Godber, then rector of Winterborne Came.[99] Although regular repairs were carried out to the Rectory, including major repair work at the end of the twenties to the roof rafters and walls of the house and stables and the entrance gate Barnes had wished to keep open, evidently its maintenance and upkeep was deemed too costly. [100] On 27 August 1958, a conveyance of the Rectory was made between the Lord Bishop of Salisbury, the Church Commissioners of England, John Anthony Sandbach Barkworth and others, and a new covenant drawn up. The house passed out of the ownership of the Church of England.

From then on there was a series of private often absentee owners and it was turned into lets. At the height of the Profumo Affair in the 1960s there was even a rumour that the Rectory,

---

[97] In a series of letters from Betha to Dadie Rylands. The Rylands Archive, King's College, Cambridge, GHWR/3/36/4.

[98] In a letter to Dadie Rylands from Lady Barnes dated 1953. The Rylands Archive, King's College, Cambridge, GHWR/3/23/4.

[99] Chedzoy, Alan, "Winterborne Came Rectory: the home of William Barnes," *Dorset Proceedings 123*, 2001, P.5.

[100] Survey Report, May 12 1928, under Ecclesiastical Dilapidations Measure, 1923.

among other Dorset homes, had been used as a refuge for Christine Keeler.[101]

The Rectory was put up for sale again by the Church Commissioners in 1963, but the sale was contested by the Came Estate. The sale could only go ahead on the condition that the Estate retained several acres of surrounding land including a meadow where William Barnes' donkey once grazed. The meadow was subsequently purchased from the estate by one of the later owners.

Interestingly, at the time of the sale, an appeal was launched to buy the Rectory with a budget of 20,000 pounds. The plan was to turn Came Rectory into an educational centre for local studies "drawing teachers and students interested in archaeology, natural history, and the work of Thomas Hardy and William Barnes himself." The purchase was to be one of the first of stages in a five-year development plan for the proposed centre, which would offer, among other services, a panel of expert advisers and translators and illustrative material for press, radio and television.[102]

During the 1960s and 1970s the Rectory was extensively "modernized" with adhesive parquet floors overlaying the original stone and wooden floors. The present owners have repaired the house and returned it as close as possible to its condition at the time of William Barnes. In particular, the stone floors in the hall and dining room have been restored. The front veranda, which had two glass panels, was repaired and now

---

[101] Keeler was the mistress of John Profumo, Secretary of State for War and "reputed" mistress of senior Soviet naval attaché and probable spy, Yevgeny Ivanov.

[102] *Country Life*, September 5, 1963, P.564.

appears as it was when it was first built. The fake Purbeck random stone columns have been replaced by rustic poles that echo the original design of cottage orné.

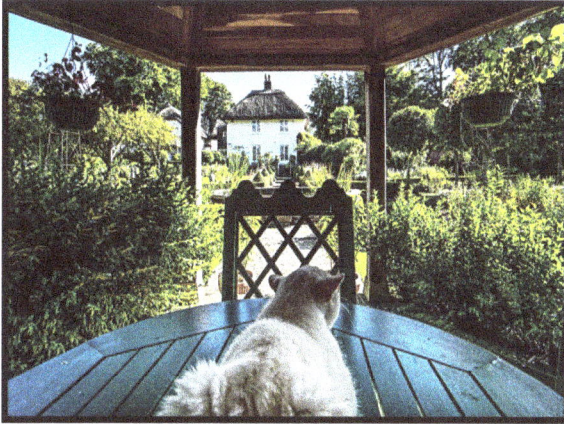

Came Today

Came Rectory was acquired by the present owners, Phil Leach and Warren Davis in 1998. As Warren recalls, they had been looking at properties all over Dorset, when they found out Came Rectory was up for sale. "Of course," says Warren, "I knew of its cultural importance, but it wasn't just that."

As former press secretary of the National Trust, Warren had leapt at the chance to own William Barnes' historic home. On a personal note, Warren is fond of recalling how his own family history is entwined with that of Came Rectory and the "big house."

"After leaving school," says Warren, "my maternal grandfather and grandmother went to work for the Seymour Damers at Came House. My grandfather was a stable boy. My grandmother worked as a maid. It was there that they met and fell in love...

"Meanwhile, my paternal grandfather, that is Walter Davis lived in Glyde Path Road in Dorchester. Hardy aficionados will know: prior to moving to Max Gate in 1885, Hardy rented a house in the same street..."

"My grandfather," Warren reminds me, "was on more than nodding acquaintance with the poet. He and Hardy used to meet in the Dorset Museum Reading Room to play chess."

"Now did you know," says Warren, who has a discursive mind, "William Barnes used to own a lathe?"

"A lathe?"

"He used the lathe to make his own chess pieces."[103]

As we sit in the dining room that was once the kitchen where the Barnes cook, Mrs. Charles would direct her staff and Tommy, the cat enters to plant himself beside Warren, the thought strikes me I will never cease to wonder at the many faceted talents of the Reverend William Barnes, who has bequeathed to us the spirit of his Dorset home.

FINIS

---

[103]Leader Scott (Baxter, Lucy), *The life of William Barnes, Poet and Philologist*, 1887, P.33.

Bibliography

The Old Rectory, Jennings, Anthony, Bloomsbury Publishing, 2009.

The Life of William Barnes, Poet and Philologist, Leader Scott (Baxter, Lucy), Macmillan and Co, 1887.

The Dorset William Barnes, Finchy, F.S., The Dorset Bookshop, 1966.

William Barnes of Dorset, Dugdale, Giles, London, Cassell & Company Ltd, London, 1953.

William Barnes, A Life of the Dorset Poet, Chedzoy, Alan, Dovecote Press Ltd, 1985.

The People's Poet, William Barnes of Dorset, Chedzoy, Alan, The History Press, 2010.

William Barnes, The Schoolmaster, Hearl, T.W., The Friary Press by Longmans (Dorchester) Ltd, 1966.

The Dorset Engravings, Barnes, William & Lindgren, Charlotte, Dorset Natural History and Archaeological Society, 1986.

The Somerset Engravings, Barnes, William & Keen, Laurence, Somerset County Council, 1989.

Kilvert's Diary, 1870-79, Kilvert, Francis, ed. Plomer, William, Book Club Associates, London, 1986.

Dorset, Mee, Arthur, Hodder and Staughton, 1939.

Thatched Buildings of Dorset, Billet, Michael, Hale Ltd, 1984.

The English Parsonage in the Early Nineteenth Century, Brittain-Catlin, Timothy, Shire Books, 2008.

Highways and Byways in Dorset, Treves, Sir Frederick, Macmillan and Co, 1935.

The Victorians, Wilson, A.N., Hutchinson, 2004.

The Collected Poems of Thomas Hardy, Wordsworth Poetry Library, 1994.

Thomas Hardy, A Biography, Millgate, Michael, 1982.

The Older Hardy, Gittings, Robert, Heinemann, 1978.

Thomas Hardy, the World of His Novels, Bullen, J.B., Francis Lincoln Limited, 2013.

The Rubáiyát of Omar Khayyam, Fitzgerald, Edward, 1859.

The Undertones of War, Blunden, Edmund, 1930.

T. E. Lawrence, Biography of a Broken Hero, Orlans, Harold, McFarland, 2002.

TE Lawrence and his Circle, Knight, Ronald D., Bat and Ball Press, 1988.

Siegfried Sassoon's Diaries, 1923-5, ed. Hart Davies, Rupert, Faber & Faber, 1983.

Goodbye to All That, Graves, Robert, Jonathan Cape, 1929.

Up The Line to Death, The War Poets, 1914-1918, ed. Gardner, Brian; foreword by Blunden, Edmund, Metheun, 1964.

A Room of One's Own, Woolf, Virginia, Oxford World's Classics, New Edition, 2015.

Barnes' Works

A mathematical investigation of the principles of hanging doors, gates, swing bridges, 1835.

Elements of Linear Perspective, 1842.

Poems of Rural Life in the Dorset Dialect, 1844.

Se Gefylsta: An Anglo-Saxon Delectus, 1849.

A Philological Grammar, grounded upon English, and formed from a Comparison of More than Sixty Languages, 1854.

Notes on Ancient Britain and the Britons, 1858.

Views of Labour and Gold, 1859.

Hwomely Rhymes, 1859.

Poems of Rural Life in the Dorset Dialect, 1862.

A Grammar and Glossary of the Dorset Dialect, 1864.

Poems of Rural Life in Common English, Massachusetts, 1869.

An outline of English Speech-Craft, C. Kegan Paul & Co, 1878.

A Glossary of the Dorset Dialect with Grammar of its Word Shapening and Wording, Dorchester, 1886.

The Poems of William Barnes. Volumes I & II, ed. Jones, Bernard, Centaur Classics, 1962.

Notable Figures in this Book

(Facing Page: from left to right)

(1) Mrs Fitzherbert (1756-1837), secret wife of George, Prince of Wales, later, George IV.
(2) Coventry Patmore (1823-96), friend of William Barnes, critic and poet best known for his narrative poem, *An Angel in the House* (1854).
(3) William Allingham (1824-89), friend of Barnes and poet, best known for his posthumously published *Diary* (1907).
(4) Seymour Dawson Damer (1832-92), pupil of Barnes, politician and benefactor.
(5) Louis Lucien Bonaparte (1813-1891), nephew to the Emperor Napoleon Bonaparte and philologist.
(6) Alfred Lord, Tennyson (1809-92), Victorian Poet laureate, author of *Idylls of the King* (1859-85), *Ulysses* (1842) and *The Charge of the Light Brigade* (1854).
(7) Francis Kilvert (1840-1879), friend of Barnes, author of *Kilvert's Diary* (1870-79).
(8) Frederick Treves (1853-1923), pupil of Barnes, surgeon and author of *The Elephant Man and Other Reminiscences* (1923).
(9) Arthur Quiller Couch (1863-1944), critic and author of *The Oxford Book of English Verse, 1250-1900* (1900).
(10) Thomas Hardy (1840-1928), friend of William Barnes, lyric poet and novelist; author of many books, including *Tess of the D'Ubervilles* (1891) and *Jude the Obscure* (1895).
(11) Edmund Gosse (1849-1928), lifelong friend of Thomas Hardy and author of *Father and Son* (1907).
(12) Francis Turner Palgrave (1824-97), poet, critic and compiler of *The Golden Treasury of English Song and Verse* (1861).
(13) Siegfried Sassoon (1886-1967), war poet, diarist, and author of *Memoirs of a Fox-hunting Man* (1928).
(14) Edmund Blunden (1896-1974), First World War poet, cricket fan, and author of *The Undertones of War* (1928).
(15) Maynard Keynes (1883-1946), celebrated economist of the post-war settlement and author of *The General Theory of Employment, Interest and Money* (1936).
(16) T.E. Lawrence "of Arabia" (1888-1935), friend to Thomas and Florence Hardy, war hero, and author of *The Seven Pillars of Wisdom* (1922).

Rosa Alba Semi-plena

Appendix 1

Julia's Rose

In his book on social economics, *Labour and Gold*, Barnes inserts a passage outlining his delight in gardening, a passion which he shared with his wife, Julia Miles:

> The sun was just below the horizon and the dew was already in the smooth, green walks, bordered by sweet smelling roses and carnations... I sat down on a rude seat I had formed beneath some old trees... I thought of the fruit and plants that were ripening around me. I exclaimed to myself "O Fortunatos, sua si bona norint, agricolas!" How happy, if they but knew their bliss, are they who till the ground.[104]

---

[104] Quoted in *William Barnes of Dorset*, Dougdale, Giles, Cassell & Company, 1953, P. 96-7.

Below is a list of potential candidates for Julia's rose, the rose Barnes brought from his Dorchester home in South Street to Came Rectory, in memory of his beloved wife.

Julia Miles died in June 1852; Barnes did not move to Came Rectory for another ten years. Candidates for Julia's rose have been chosen on the basis that they would have been grown prior to the 1850s, although the rose may well have been one Barnes grew after Julia's death in the 1850s but prior to his move to Came Rectory in the early 1860s. The literature suggests that Julia's rose was a pure white rose, possibly with a yellow tint. The flower was not "mossed" with abundant petals like the Alba Massima, but a bloom with fewer petals such as the Alba Semi-plena. It also seems likely that the rose was early blooming like the Burnet Double White, since Barnes' favourite season was spring, the season of the "growth of plants" and "the unfolding of blossoms."[105]

The roses listed below are all shrub as opposed to climbing roses from *The Peter Beales Collection*.[106]

---

[105] Quoted in *William Barnes of Dorset*, Dougdale, Giles, Cassell & Company, 1953, P. 96-7.

[106] Classic Roses, *The Peter Beales Collection for 2004-2005*, printed by Crowes Complete Print of Norwich.

Rose	Description	Date
Blanche de Vilbert	Cupped flower opening flat and fully double	1847
Burnet Double White Scotch Rose	Early flowering, small round blackish hips in autumn	Pre-1650
Mme Bravy	Creamy white with pink shadings and strong fragrance	1846
Blanchefleur	Very double, sweetly scented with occasional pink tints	1835
Botzaris	Sweet damask scent with fully double, quartered flowers of creamy white	1856
Mme Hardy	Very fragrant and double with a green button eye	1832
Quatre Saisons Blanc Mousseaux	Well mossed bud opening to fully double, white scented flowers	Old, date unknown

Shailer's White Moss, "White Bath"	Profusely mossed and fragrant	1788
White Provence, "Unique Blanche"	Creamy white, late flowering, silky texture	1775
Alba Maxima, "Jacobite Rose", "White Rose of York"	White with creamy tinted centre. Good autumn fruit	C16th
Blanche de Belgique	Pure white with superb perfume	1817
Alba Semi-plena	Semi double pure white flowers, sweetly scented	C16th or earlier
Jeanne d'Arc	Muddled cream fragrant flowers fade to white in hot sun	1818
Mme. Legras de St. Germain	Almost thornless rose of creamy white	1846
Mme. Plantier	Double creamy white, fairly early summer	1835

Appendix 2

Siegfried Sassoon's letter to Bernard Jones

Hysterbury House 5/4/59

Dear Mr Jones

Various distractions have prevented me answering your letter sooner, and even now I don't feel capable of replying at any great length, though I fully share and sympathize with your interest in Barnes and T.H. – as needs no saying!

As you know I was at Max Gate frequently during the last nine years of his life. But at that time I was only beginning to appreciate Barnes and I have done since. I did try to draw him out about W.B, assuming it to be a favourite subject with him. But for some reason he seemed unwilling to say much, probably because he preferred to discuss the modern poets with whom he liked to feel in touch. Possibly he was tired of being asked about his old friend.

Mrs Hardy arranged for E.B and 2 to stay as paying guests, at Came Rectory, in July, 1923, so that we could be within easy reach of Max Gate. EB was much more of an authority on Barnes' poems than I. I have all the editions of them, including Edward Fitzgerald's copy of the 1844 volume, and also a notebook of W.B.'s containing notes of Anglo-Saxon lectures taken when he was at Halle Univ. Germany in 1842 — a detail which is not mentioned in his daughter's biography. —

I am afraid this is all the information I can offer.
With all good wishes,
Yours sincerely,
Siegfried Sassoon.

Photos and Drawings

The images in this book have been created from digital photos either held in the public domain or under Creative Commons Attribution Share Alike licenses. The author would like to express his enthusiasm and appreciation of all those who of all those who donate their work to Creative Commons and whose work is celebrated here.

The following licenses are referred to in the notes below:
CC BY-SA 2.0: Attribution Share Alike Generic
(www. creativecommons.org/licenses/by-sa/2.0/legalcode)
CC BY-SA 3.0: Attribution Share Alike Unported
(www. creativecommons.org/licenses/by-sa/3.0/legalcode)
CC BY-SA 4.0: Attribution Share Alike International
(www. creativecommons.org/licenses/by-sa/4.0/legalcode)

(1) Front Cover: derivative of drawing of Came Rectory, donated by Warren Davis; derivative of Maple Leaf Structure (2008) by Steve Jurvetson under CC BY-SA 2.0. Cropped, overlaid and scaled from originals by S. Proctor.

(2) Back Cover: Barnes family and grandchildren, Dorset County Museum Archive; Came Rectory Garden today. Photo donated by Warren Davis. Scaled and overlaid from originals with border.

(3) Derivative of Tyche, public domain. Cropped, scaled and overlaid from original with border.

(4) Derivative of Came Rectory (2015) by Christopher Middleton. Photo donated by Warren Davis. Cropped, scaled and overlaid from original with border.

(5) Derivative of William Barnes (1870s), photographer unknown, Dorset County Museum Archive. Cropped and scaled from original with border.

(6) Derivative of detail from a watercolour by a friend of Mr. Davis. Cropped and scaled from original with border.

(7) Derivative of The Musicians, a leaf from William Barnes' Sketch Book, given by Major Lawrance Barnes, the poet's grandson to Captain B. C. Williams, 13 September, 1924.Scaled and overlaid from original with border.

(8) Derivative of engraving of a woman milking a cow, William Barnes (1830s). Cropped, scaled and overlaid from original with border.

(9) Derivative of Old Came Rectory with Laura Barnes gardening (1880s), Dorset County Museum Archive. Scaled and overlaid from original with border.

(10) Derivative of Henry Moule's earth closet, improved version, ca 1875 (2008) by Musphot under CC BY-SA 3.0. Scaled and overlaid from original with border.

(11) Derivative of Thomas Hardy (1889) by Herbert Rose Berraud, public domain,

and William Barnes (ca 1870s), Dorset County Museum Archive. Scaled and overlaid from originals with borders.

(12) Derivative of illustration from A Book of Nursery Rhymes (1901) by Clare T. Atwood, public domain. Scaled and overlaid from original with border.

(13) Derivative of Domestic Staff at Came Rectory, centre, Mrs Charles, cook (1880); Aunt Laura Barnes, date unknown Ethel and Arthur, William Barnes' grandchildren. Scaled and overlaid with from originals with borders.

(14) Derivative of: after wedding of Isabel Shaw (nee Barnes) to Thomas Gardener, 17 October, 1882: Constance, Reverend William Barnes, Arthur on donkey (Tom?), Harry Gardner, Ethel, Aunt Laura, Annette Gardner and (?), Dorset County Museum Archive. Cropped, scaled and overlaid from original.

(15) Derivative of William Barnes' bed shortly after his death, Dorset County Museum Archive. Scaled and overlaid from original with border.

(16) The War Poets, derivative of Siegfried Sassoon (1915) by George Charles Beresford, public domain, and Edmund Blunden (ca 1914), author unknown, public domain. Scaled and overlaid from originals with border.

(17) Derivative of T.E. Lawrence on his Brough Superior (1920s), public domain. Scaled and overlaid from original with border.

(18) Derivative of Moving Finger (Quatrain 50), illustration to Rubáiyát of Omar Khayyam (pre-1930), Edmund J Sullivan, public domain. Scaled and overlaid from original with border.

(19) Derivative of Came Garden with Tommy the cat (2015) by Christopher Middleton. Photo donated by. Scaled and overlaid from original with border.

(20) Derivative of illustration from Tennyson's Idylls of the King (1867) by Gustav Doré, public domain. Scaled and overlaid from original with border.

(21) From left to right: derivatives of the following images are in the public domain except where stated: portrait of Mrs Fitzherbert, wife of George IV (early C19th), in the manner of George Romney, date unknown; Coventry Patmore (no later than 1905), author unknown; William Allingham (1908), engraving by Emery Walker; Lionel Seymour Dawson Damer (1871) by James Tissot, Vanity Fair; Louis Lucien Bonaparte (mid-C19th), public domain; Alfred Lord, Tennyson with book (May 1865) by Julia Margaret Cameron; Francis Kilvert (1870s), author unknown; Sir Frederick Treves (1884), lithograph, Wellcome Images under CC BY-SA 4.0; photo of Arthur Quiller Couch (no later than 1895), author unknown; portrait of Sir Edmund Gosse (1886) by John Singer Sargent; Thomas Hardy (1889) by Herbert Rose Berraud; Francis Palgrave (1872) by Samuel Lawrence; Siegfried Sassoon (1915) by George Charles Beresford; Edmund Blunden (ca 1914), author unknown; Maynard Keynes (1934), caricature by David Low; Thomas Edward Lawrence by Augustus John (1919). Scaled and overlaid from originals with borders.

(22) Derivative of Rosa Alba Semi-plena (1988) by A. Barra under CA BY-SA 3.0. Scaled and overlaid from original.

(23) Derivative of Barnes' Cupid, Dorset County Museum Archive. Scaled and overlaid from original with border.

ABOUT THE AUTHOR

Born in Poole, Dorset, Sedley Proctor grew up in London and was educated in Winchester and Nottingham. In the 1990s, he worked in fringe theatre. For the best part of two decades, he lived and worked as a teacher and translator in Southern Italy. Author of *The Half Days* (2015), Sedley also writes, with Tony Henderson, under the pen-name Peter & Paul. Together they have published two books: *Over & Under i* (2015) and *Over & Under ii* (2016).

www.ingramcontent.com/pod-product-compliance
Lightning Source LLC
Chambersburg PA
CBHW041928040426

42443CB00019B/3499